DICTIONARY OF DOODLES

Gloria Hargreaves

W. Foulsham & Co. Ltd.

London • New York • Toronto • Cape Town • Sydney

W. Foulsham & Company Limited
Yeovil Road, Slough, Berkshire, SL1 4JH

ISBN 0–572–01480–5

Printed in Great Britain at St. Edmundsbury Press,
Bury St. Edmunds.

Contents

Contents

Contents

What's in a doodle?

Most doodles are produced unconsciously on shopping lists, magazines, blotting sheets, shorthand books, but most frequently on telephone pads. Because they are often scribbled whilst we are thinking of something quite different they are good indicators of our hidden desires, aspirations, feelings or anxieties. The doodle on a telephone pad not only whiles away the time spent waiting to speak to someone (or waiting for them to come to the point) – it's also a great tension reliever and enables us to get rid of our pent-up feelings. Indeed, psychologists see doodles as a projection of hidden emotions and they are often used in personality assessment.

Some of us doodle just occasionally; others constantly. Many people believe they never doodle – that is, until they look at their telephone pad!

Collect all your doodles together – check the shape, form, line, movement. A scribble, a dot, a line or a full graphic picture – all have their own particular interpretation. Check out your own doodles in the book using the category listings, but don't be surprised if they aren't identical reproductions – everyone doodles in a slightly different way and some of the doodles here are shown in their most detailed form, purely to help give an accurate analysis. Use the guidelines overleaf for further enlightenment on your own doodling style.

You may well produce a variety of types – some showing aggression, others perhaps indicating a romantic nature. This need not surprise you when you think what a mixture of traits go to make-up our own individual personality. Obviously, if you produce the same doodle constantly, this will indicate a dominant trait;

others produced occasionally may just suggest a sudden bout of, for example, passion or temper.

These doodles are all about YOU. What motivates you, is it sex, money, power, greed? I guarantee you will be amazed just how much you can learn about yourself and your unconscious mind. Try it out on your friends, too, it could well make for greater understanding.

Positioning

The position of the doodles on the page has its own particular significance.
Centre page – this suggests you are extroverted and need to be noticed.
Right-hand side – tomorrow is what matters to you, you want to get on with living.
Left-hand side – the past has a strong hold on you, break free!
Top of the page – you are over enthusiastic, come down-to-earth a little.
Bottom of the page – you are being negative. Cheer-up, it might never happen!

Shading

Shading-in can indicate anxiety, tension and even depression.

Retracing

This indicates a certain compulsiveness in your personality structure.

You need to relax a little and let go at the appropriate time.

Pressure

Pressure can be tested by feeling the indentation at the back of the page between your forefinger and thumb. The greater the indentation the heavier the pressure. Medium leaves a slight indentation and light cannot be felt.

Heavy shows a great deal of energy and some aggression.
Medium – the most common form – indicates a balanced personality.
Light shows sensitivity but an inability to absorb experiences.
Erratic shows a very changeable nature, happy one minute, miserable the next.

Writing Implement

Black: can be artistic but also slightly depressive.
Blue: a need for harmony in your surroundings.
Red: a sign of energy and a vivacious personality.
Green: you are slightly eccentric and can be resentful.
Brown: rarely seen these days. You are an earthy, practical type.
These interpretations are only valid if you deliberately pick one of these colours rather than use what is readily available.

Abstract

Step-like movements show some leadership qualities. Although the whole suggests ambition, you are reasonably flexible and open to suggestion. Likely to reach the top of your profession with an ability to be tough sometimes, kindly at other times, and the wisdom to know which is appropriate and when.

You are a very precise and exacting individual who tackles one problem at a time. There is a definite pattern to this behaviour, making you very predictable but also utterly reliable and quite determined. You leave nothing to chance.

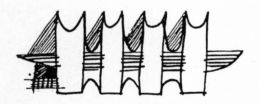

Abstract

A very gentle person who 'rides on the crest of a wave', you speak ill of no-one nor will believe unsavoury rumours spread by anyone else. A true romantic who sees good in one and all.

Insecurity is shown here, the doodle of a gentle person who is feeling angry and then reverts to normal soft nature. It suggest uncertainty about the future and difficulty in reaching a decision. It could also indicate that you have been made angry by a decision forced upon you.

Abstract

Firm strokes here show a positive attitude, while the filling-in shows some tension. There is a lot of originality in these doodles indicating a fertile mind. The sharp strokes show you can be critical, and will fight hard to achieve your aims in life. The second doodle shows that subconsciously you want to spread your wings a little.

Abstract

There are a lot of angular movements here showing determination and the desire to succeed. Even the heart is vaguely angular and the diamond on top is very sharp. You have almost certainly suffered a broken heart recently and you are determined not to leave yourself wide open to such an eventuality again.

Taken as a whole the doodle suggests you are temporarily adopting a very hard attitude but would like to be softer and more romantic.

Intricate Patterns

Intricate doodles are the type you find
in the boardroom. When people are
under pressure their doodles become
more and more involved, indicating
uncertainty or insecurity (and the larger
the doodle the greater the insecurity).

The repetition in the doodles on the
right show a compulsiveness in your
character. You can invariably be relied
on to speak your mind and you are
inclined to be easily irritated.

Repetitive Patterns

This doodling habit shows discontent and some form of obsessional behaviour. You are probably a pedantic person and a poor delegator who feels no-one else can do a job properly.

Angular repetitive patterns are a sign that great feelings of anger are being concealed. You are likely to explode with rage if not invited to voice your opinions. You also have a tendency to look for something to be annoyed about!

Retracing Patterns

Any form of retracing is a sign of anxiety and tension. It often occurs when you are under pressure and over-worked. Poor delegators frequently retrace. If it persists, it should be taken as a warning to slow down.

Aerials

This doodle is characteristic of someone with many ideas who is trying hard to clarify them. You are building up your ideas as you go along and changing your plans where appropriate.

A determination to put all these plans on a firm footing is shown by the brick chimney and roof top.

Airplanes

These are the sign of a freedom seeker. You are a dreamer who longs for faraway places, with a desire to escape temporarily from all responsibilities.

The more detailed your doodle, the greater your need to get away from it all.

(Pilots and people related to the aircraft industry do also tend to produce these doodles with no particularly significant meaning other than a sense of involvement).

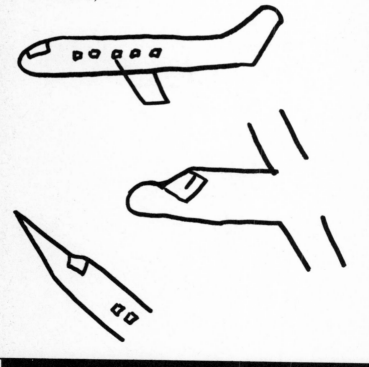

Airplanes

A definite desire to escape from present surroundings. All three are pointing downwards – evidence of slight depression. You are an adventurous character who needs freedom to follow your ideas. The attention to detail is excellent – a sign of good powers of concentration.

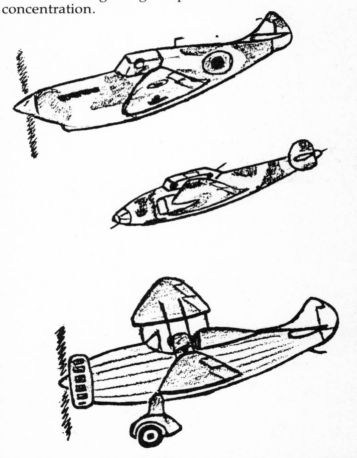

Angles

What a determined person you are!
Any angular movement whether it
appears in doodles, or handwriting,
shows an inflexible attitude to life.
Undoubtedly, you have a keen mind
and a critical one but the complexities
of human emotion just baffle you. You
rely on facts and facts alone!

Arches

You have a tendency to be secretive
plus a dislike of being questioned about
behaviour or movements. Honest and
reliable, you take life seriously and
have a strong respect for others.
Always loyal to family and friends, you
also have a healthy respect for
tradition.

The shape still suggests a shielding of
thoughts and ideas (see above), while
the addition of the flowers indicates
you have a gentle personality. You are
friendly and good-humoured, with a
willingness to help others less fortunate
than yourself.

Arrows

A doodle of straightforward arrows is a
sign of the calculating mind. You are
also the sort of person who enjoys
dealing with life's problems.

Should you keep adding heads until the
whole arrow is filled – then you are
very persistent indeed and may even
seek problems before they arrive on
your door-step.

An arrow with an inner circle shows
you may take a softer line, but the
repeated strokes of the arrow head are
an indication of firmness and definite
ideas.

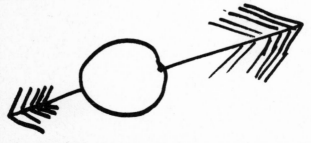

Arrows

An arrow with a square base shows you are an intelligent, imaginative individual with many ideas, all based on a solid foundation.

If you favour this type of arrow you are a clear, concise and to-the-point type of person who enjoys handling other peoples' problems, but does so in a gentle manner.

If this double-headed arrow is your hallmark, you are an imaginative type who slows down to ensure his ideas are based on sound common sense.

You are undoubtedly an ambitious person who has difficulty in delegating. The circle at the centre suggests self, while the arrows show ambition and drive. The dots around the edge suggest you want to remain in control at all times. This is quite a positive doodle, the firm strokes showing a lot of determination.

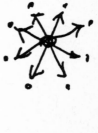

Arrows

Another example of a calculating mind, but tempered with more caution. You are very exacting and must know all the facts. Lawyers and solicitors produce these – if you aren't one, perhaps you should think of a change of career! This type of cased arrow is the doodle of a very progressive individual. You like to reach the core of all problems and love giving advice.

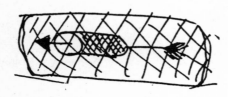

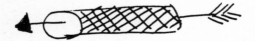

Arrows

The double-headed arrows going in all
directions show you are a go-getter but
wondering which direction to take. The
shading-in is a sign of tension and
nervousness – you are about to make a
decision and are hoping that it is the
right one.

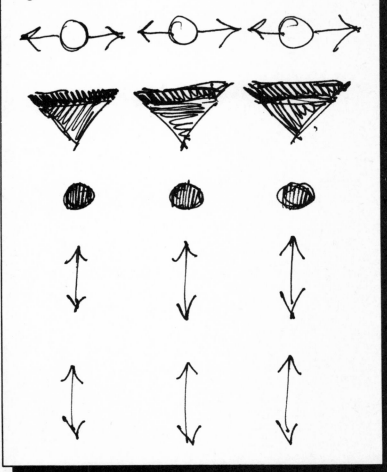

Arrow Suit

Frustration is evident here, along with the desire to escape. You have an intelligent, calculating mind but the two-way arrows are a sign that you are not making much progress. A thwarted individual, you feel as if you are taking one step forward and two steps back.

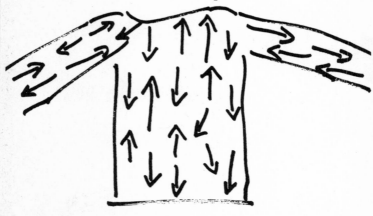

Ball and Chain

What a heavy weight! Life is just too restricting for you and you are hoping for someone to sort out your problems for you. Not a happy person, you are prone to making heavy work of minor set-backs.

Ball and chain doodlers tend to go over the ball again and again showing a great degree of depression at the time.

Baskets

A basket-doodler is generally open to
new ideas with a desire to make
progress. If your basket is open, you
are a receptive, friendly type who is
always willing to learn.

A basket with a half-open lid suggests
you are not too sure about advice
given. You have a tendency to query
and question the motives of others.
Your desire to learn is tempered by
selectiveness in what you absorb.

Bells

1. You have an awareness of time and a desire to please others, although you are guilty of immaturity and childishness as well! A bell doodle can also indicate a possessive attitude towards home and family.

2. If your bell is shaded, you are feeling rushed and depressed. Time seems to be running out and the tasks in hand are not yet finished. The roundness is a sign of some immature behavioural patterns.

3. If your bell has a chunky handle, then you can be counted on for solid ideas and an awareness of time. You will meet your schedules on time no matter how hard you have to work.

3.

1.

2.

Beer Mugs

You think of yourself as a great ladies man, imagining that all the women you meet are swooning at your feet. To you, a friendly smile means "my place, or yours"! You're not particularly offensive, however, you just like to feel good in front of your mates.

Bird House

The angular movements here show determination and some aggression. Not a person to be a pushed around, you put up a good argument when you feel you are right. Quite a practical personality.

Your high ideals cause you to set high standards for yourself and others. Quite ambitious and intelligent, you tend not to be terribly practical. In fact, you're a bit of a dreamer.

Birds

Intelligent and imaginative, you also have a demanding conscience, with very clear-cut views on what is right and what is wrong. A clear thinker, you plan your time well.

You are broadminded with a love of large spaces in which to spread yourself. A good traveller, you are also tolerant – this is the doodle of a freedom lover!

The doodle of a clear-thinking loner. The economical lines are evidence of a strong dislike of clutter. Slightly slow when making decisions you always stand by what you eventually decide.

Birds

Gulls

A very common one and the sign of a relaxed, easy going and communicative person.

Re-tracing of the same one shows irritation and the desire to speed things up a little: it is probably for those reasons that these are most often produced on a telephone pad!

Blind

This is characteristic of someone who hides all their own thoughts whilst taking note of everything going on around them. The office gossip for example – could this be you?

Want to know anything about anyone? Then just ask this doodler!

A **chess board** doodle shows a very competitive streak. Its squareness shows a materialistic tendency, and you are inclined to fluctuate between periods of elation and deflation.

Snakes and ladders – you're the type of person who wants to reach the top rung of the ladder even if you have to be ruthless. Indicative of a big ego.

A **number board** shows you are a solid type, interested in hard facts. You welcome straight, clear-cut dealings whether in your business or emotional life.

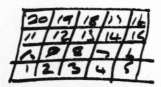

Boats

Habitual boat doodlers are exhibiting a
desire for freedom and a longing to
escape from their present environment.
However, you may also produce these
doodles when a holiday is imminent
and you are looking forward to a
change of surroundings.

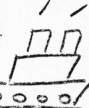

Books

The open page shows a thirst for
knowledge and its simplicity shows you
are one who sees essentials and acts
upon them.

A closed book indicates a secretive
nature as well as a love of facts.

If you favour a row of books, you like
to work in a methodical manner but
have a tendency to show-off your
knowledge.

Building books in step form shows you
have a constructive mind. It also
indicates ambition and the desire to
reach the top of your profession.

You need a prop! You must learn to
stand on your own two feet and not
run to others every time you have a
problem.

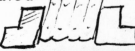

Brick Wall

You like possessions and the security and protection they bring. Practical and methodical, you are also stubborn.

A less methodical character than the doodler above, you are prepared to take more risks to achieve your aims; your ideas, however, are founded on a solid basis.

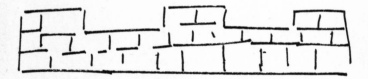

Butterflies

You tend to be a sensitive person, but one who does not get involved in anything too deeply. You flit from relationship to relationship with complete ease; likewise your interests and hobbies are constantly changing. Although you are a delighful companion, others must not take you too seriously or expect anything long-term from a relationship with you.

Cats

If you doodle helpless animals it shows
a romantic nature and a kindness of
spirit. The lack of face here shows
some dissatisfaction with your own
self-image. The curly tail is evidence
of a good sense of humour.

A romantic, gentle type, a lover of all
small animals and helpless people, you
may well have a cosseted pet of your
own. You hate friction or aggression,
and you are easily hurt. A very good
neighbour and friend, you are always
prepared to do a good deed.

Cell Bars

You are quite obviously trapped in something which you find both irritating and frustrating. You would like to spread your wings and be off as far away as possible. Critical and sarcastic, you loathe any form of criticism directed towards yourself.

Chinese Figures

You aren't a particularly trustworthy individual, I'm afraid. You have a devious side and find no difficulty in bending the rules and even less difficulty in justifying your behaviour.

A row of figures really just reinforces the comments above. You believe rules are meant to be broken and you'll break the lot as and when you think fit!

Circles

If you are a doodler of circles, you can congratulate yourself on being a flexible individual. However, this is the lazy persons doodle; little effort is required here. You are not particularly energetic and rarely put up a fight for what you believe in, although you are often helpful to others.

If the circles are stacked or linked you may well succeed in your aims by being very amiable and pleasant – doing your utmost to avoid any sort of aggression.

A row of circles shows a sense of order – you perform your duties in a gentle manner, without rushing.

Doodling patterned circles indicates you are a soft, pleasant type with imagination but lacking in drive. If your circles have equal divisions you are secretive about your movements and hate being questioned about your moods or motives. However, you do have a love of order and a sense of fairplay.

Clocks

A straightforward clock shows you are very frequently late for appointments but always apologise profusely. Others find it difficult to be angry with you because you always seem to have such a good excuse!

You always *try* to be on time, but don't always succeed! You do, at least, have every intention of improving your ways.

Square clock doodlers are sticklers for timekeeping. You can't abide anyone turning up late for an appointment – you yourself are always there five minutes before time.

Clouds

If you favour light, fluffy clouds you
have an amiable disposition and are
invariably helpful, kind and
sympathetic. Pleasant to everyone, you
are nice to have around.

Tension is showing here – you suffer
from major swings of mood. You can
be hard to understand, rarely reacting
the same way to similar situations.

You tend to start the day on top of the
world and finish it in a deep fit of
depression. Furthermore, once
depressed you don't really want to be
cheered-up.

Clowns

You are a very cheerful, humorous individual who enjoys play-acting and drawing attention to yourself. Always good for a laugh, you enjoy telling stories – usually wildly embroidered – which can be quite vulgar!

This type of clown doodle shows you would like to be taken more seriously. You play the idiot but resent the fact that you have to be funny for people to notice you. There are signs that you have an inferiority complex.

Cotton Reels

Cotton reel doodlers take a broad view of the world and want to know and see everything. They have a love of the arts and want freedom to follow their own talents. However, they also tend to be impressionable, undisciplined and somewhat unpredictable.

A big ego is shown here – lots of self-confidence. Also an ambitious character (the taller the spikes, the greater the ambition). Many leadership qualities are in evidence as is a critical nature (shown by the spikes).

Crown of thorns

If you doodle something like this you are showing a morbid fascination with death. You have a strong dislike of self combined with an unhappy nature. You tend to see everything in shades of black and white and you can be very intolerant of your fellow human beings.

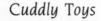

Cuddly Toys

Such doodles show you have an affectionate, warm nature. You love a cuddle and are demonstrative in your displays of affection.

You make a good friend and are always ready to help. However, you tend to be a chatterbox. You also hate being left alone for too long.

Dartboard

You are the sort who sets yourself a target and does your utmost to achieve it. Your competitive nature thrives on a challenge. Calculating, strong-minded and ambitious, you can actually become quite depressed if you do not achieve your goals.

Diamonds

Doodling diamonds is an indication of a penetrating mind – you are curious and like to know the answers to sometimes inexplicable things.

A pattern of diamonds with an upward point shows a logic that is aggressive and energetic.

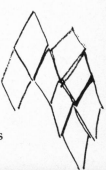

The downward pointing pattern is a sign of energy directed to experiences of a physical and personal nature.

Dice

A down-to-earth personality, you have some degree of adventure in your spirit. You will take a chance once you have calculated the odds. You don't take too many risks but you do play to win.

Dogs

Dog doodlers exhibit similar characteristics to cat doodlers. You are a romantic type with a strong dislike of any form of aggression.

Bared teeth on the animal could well indicate subconscious fear of all dogs.

Dots

You display two main characteristics –
you are cautious and think before you
speak but nevertheless you always have
the need to say the last word.

If the dots are joined up in any way
you are subconsciously linking your
ideas together.

Egg Timer

This doodle shows you are the sort of
person who always intends to be on
time, but never quite manages it. It is
also produced by men or women who
feel they are losing the "first flush of
youth" and don't like it.

If you doodle a more angular version
you are a stickler for good time-keeping
and are likely to get quite angry if you
are kept waiting.

Elephant

A good sense of humour is shown here plus a slightly devious nature. You make your own rules and don't always tell the truth.

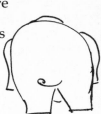

Envelopes

Envelope doodles have a variety of meanings

Blank – you are awaiting the arrival of a letter.

Blank and narrow – you are awaiting the letter's arrival but fearful of the content.

Writing to the far right – you are impulsive and escaping the past.

Writing to the far left – you are clinging to the past and frightened of change.

Writing in the centre – you are co-operative and well organised.

Writing very low down – you are depressed and pessimistic.

Eyes

A preoccupation with doodling eyes is the sign of a rather self-centred nature. Although self-absorbed, however, you are inclined to be emotionally out-of-touch with yourself.

Seeking answers, the face-to-face confrontation doodle indicates a desire to talk some of your problems through.

This detailed and rather sultry eye with large lashes is the doodle of a flirtatious person. You are quite likely to dress in a provocative manner but show complete amazement if someone were to make an improper suggestion!

Faces

A half face or one drawn in profile is a
definite indication that you are hiding
something. You have an inability to
face reality – perhaps you cannot bear
to admit to yourself that a relationship
has broken up, and you are hoping for
its resumption. The shading-in also
shows great depression.

You are feeling dissatisfied with the
situation you are in, as shown by the
dour and unfriendly face. The filled-in
petals and stems show you are feeling
both sensitive and angry at the same
time, as well as very critical.

Faces

The significance of these face doodles depends upon their shape and expression.

The smiling, rounded face shows happiness. You enjoy your family and friends and are generally sexually content.

The unhappy face reflects your inner feelings and may suggest the need for a new friend or mate!

An angular face indicates a longing for security and critical sentiments regarding your friends and family.

A long face shows you are inclined to melancholy and lacking in positive thinking.

Feet

Doodling feet of any description is an indication of sexual desires. This foot doodler is likely to be an earthy, passionate type who is not too romantic but invariably honest and direct.

Fence

Spiky fence doodles are the sign of a sarcastic person. You love to subdue others with the use of a few well-chosen caustic words.

The boarded-fence is characteristic of a self-protective nature. Although you have quite definite ideas you are generally noncommittal.

Fireplaces

You are a homelover and quite probably female. You love having your family and friends around and you are happiest when looking after others and tending to their needs.

Flags

A simple flag indicates a competitive nature and the angularity shows aggression. You tend to be brief, concise and to-the-point.

A square flag shows you are a steady, practical, person with both feet firmly on the ground.

A chequered flag is an indication of uncertainty and feeling unsure of yourself.

Heavy shading shows you are very nervous and depressed and feeling uncertain about decisions already taken. You are not a cheerful companion at this time.

Flowers

A flower doodler is likely to be a sentimental person. There is a lot of gentleness and affection in these type of movements.

You are probably very good at remembering to send birthday cards, but you feel really hurt if you are forgotten.

Fort

This shows good attention to detail and
the ability to concentrate for long
periods of time alone on a project. You
are receptive to new ideas and a
progressive thinker. Quite
broadminded, you have a healthy
respect for tradition and a distinct
dislike of clutter.

The lack of a drawbridge in this doodle
shows a more self-protective attitude.
Although you think before you speak,
you are always ready with an answer.

Cherries

Cherry doodles show a nice nature and a person who likes to plan in advance. You don't like too much rush at the last moment.

Grapes

The bunch of grapes shows a steady and methodical build-up of ideas. You are prepared to put in quite a bit of effort to achieve your aims, and you act in a careful and considered way.

Pineapple

The roundness of the pineapple suggests that you are quite charming under a touchy exterior. You have quite firm ideas and are not easily pushed around. However, you do have a tendency to cling to ideas.

Ghosts

Ghost doodles represent a fear of the unknown. They may be produced prior to going to the dentist or into hospital. Indicative of insecurity, uncertainty, fear (invariably of a temporary nature), they are often done by very shy people who loathe any situation they consider embarrassing.

Giraffe in a frame

This shows a devious nature – you tell people what you want them to know, rather than the true facts. It also shows a dislike of figures of authority.

Giraffe without a frame

This doodle shows a condescending nature – you tend to speak down to people and rarely listen to what they have to say.

Gravestones

These doodles are fairly common
during periods of deep depression.
They do not necessarily suggest suicidal
tendencies but do indicate a morbid
obsession with death. If you have been
very deeply affected by a bereavement
you may well produce such a doodle.

The shaded-in version suggests you
bear great ill-will towards others.

Hats

If you are a doodler of hats, you are probably a gentle, sensitive person. Invariably they are done with a light pressure showing a delicacy of feeling and a dislike of rudeness and loud noises.

Headgear

Although you may approach people in a friendly manner initially, you become more argumentative when you feel you are not achieving your aims. You have quite a sharp tongue and can be pretty sarcastic.

You may appear reasonable at first but you are quick to show aggression. Not one to be argued with, you like to win no matter what tactics have to be used. You enjoy subduing others with a few well-chosen words.

Argumentative, persuasive, you will not give in when you are determined to make a point. Don't start a discussion with this type unless you have a lot of time to spare!

Hearts

This sort of doodle shows a romantic
nature. You are very sentimental and in
love with the idea of being "in love."

Heart doodles are often produced after
the break-up of a relationship by the
partner who has not fully accepted the
situation.

If you include an arrow through the
heart, it could be you will fight to
regain your love.

This doodle shows you are romantic
but obsessive in love. There is no room
for anyone or anything else in your life.
You should look carefully at your
situation; it is unhealthy to see love as
possession, and this sort of love allows
no freedom for personal growth.

Hedgehog

The sign of someone who is rather prickly, like the animal. You love to criticise others but hate any form of criticism of yourself.

Know anyone in the office who is good with backhanded compliments ('You have a wonderful figure – for your age')? Then look at their notepad for a doodled hedgehog!

Horse

This is a sign of strength and power, although not so much physical strength as strength of character. You are someone others can lean on.

Horse doodles are often produced by successful people who enjoy having others look to them for guidance. Invariably they are prepared to use their powers to assist others.

Hot Air Balloon

You prefer to be on solid ground but are easily swept away with enthusiasm. An ideas person, you are happiest being innovative. Impulsive and imaginative, you have a very good chance of succeeding in your aims in life.

Houses

You are a very broadminded individual who loves large rooms and empty spaces in which to spread yourself. You see the world as a great place to explore and you want to enjoy all it has to offer. Generous in your spending, you enjoy travel from the moment you pack your bags.

Houses

You are the homely type. Possibly a bit insular, but true friends are always welcome here. A homemaker, you see your home as a place of security from the outside world.

You are very idealistic with a penetrating mind. You are always seeking answers, sometimes to the inexplicable.

Houses

A narrow-minded individual who is rather up-tight, you have very fixed ideas and no interest whatsoever in compromise. You have a cold, rather unemotional nature.

The sign of an aggressive, tense personality. The complexities of human emotion are beyond you. All appeals to you must be based on logic – you do not recognise the existence of intuition.

A tent-like affair indicates you have a constructive mind – you like to work for long periods of time alone on a project and you're not too keen on interruptions.

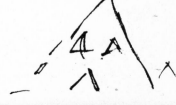

Completely rounded movements throughout indicate you have a friendly and hospitable nature. The grouping of the doodles shows a sharing of ideas. The rather large noses show a love of the good things of life and the whole suggests warmth. There is no rigidity whatsoever here suggesting a laid-back environment.

Humorous

A practical joker with a great sense of
fun, you do have quite an inflated ego
and a tendency to expect everyone to
enjoy your jokes. Nevertheless your
generous nature makes you a very
cheerful companion.

You have a tendency to tell dirty jokes!

You have a good sense of humour, and
a soft, loving nature which is not being
satisfied.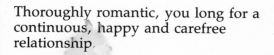

Thoroughly romantic, you long for a
continuous, happy and carefree
relationship.

Constant repetition of a similar doodle
indicates some compulsiveness. Your
hunt is on and you will continue to
seek a soft, flexible and kindly mate.

Humorous

If you produce doodles along these lines, you are generally light-headed, and always ready with a cheerful word even when you have problems yourself.

You have a lot of imagination and a flair for detail, but above all you have the ability to smile in the face of adversity

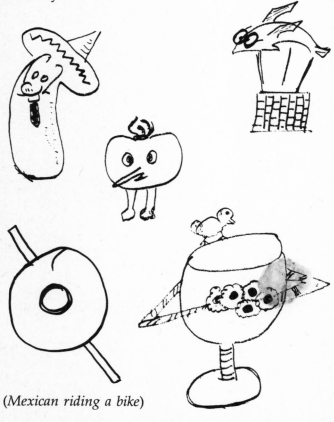

(*Mexican riding a bike*)

Humorous

1. You have an eye for detail and you enjoy working for a long time on a project. A kindly person, you are always willing to lend a helping hand. You have a very good sense of humour and a sense of the ridiculous – all in all, you are a nice person to have around!

2. Your sense of humour is tempered with a tendency to be self-critical. Although you like to crack a joke, you are never quite sure how it is going to be received.

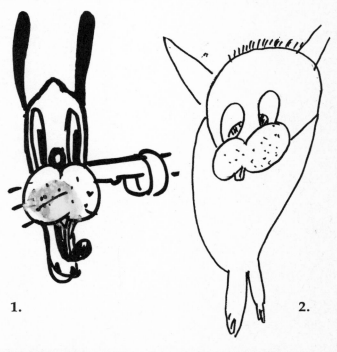

1.

2.

Humorous

You are a joker and rarely take anything seriously. People love having you around.

You like things on an even keel and once you feel secure, you are great fun to be with. However, you're not quite so cheerful when things aren't going your way.

You are a tall-story teller – no-one can believe a word you say! You love telling stories and you embroider them each time you tell them! You may be a liar, but at least you are funny with it!

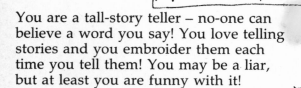

Initials

It is quite common for people to doodle their initials or those of a loved one.

Doodling your own initials is a sign of the desire to impress others. You are determined to make your mark on the world.

Doodling your partner's initials shows some insecurity about the relationship. You are wondering if they are happy with you. The larger the doodle, the greater the evidence of insecurity.

Insects

Doodling creepy-crawlies is often a sign of irritation. Where the claws or antennae are long or extended, you are showing signs of fear and a desire to avoid such insects.

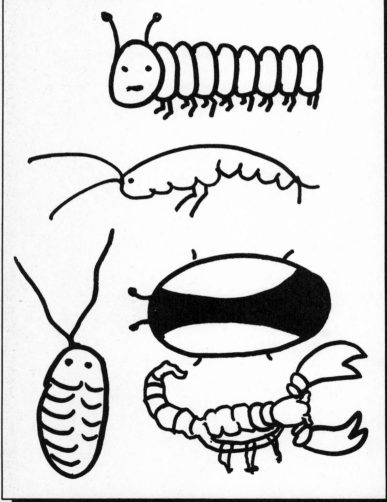

Jewellery

You are exhibiting signs of materialism and a feeling of confidence and self-worth. The more rounded the items the more romantic the feeling but nevertheless this is still a sign of acquisitiveness.

Angular items show a definite love of possessions – just for the sake of them!

Kites

If you produce something like this, you have high ideals and are literally reaching for the sky. A kite with a long string shows you are likely to achieve your aims.

A kite with a short string shows you are not sufficiently practical to put your ideas into practice.

Ladders

The sign of a social climber! You display a lot of confidence and have a well-developed ego. The higher the ladder the more ambitious you are to reach the top. You are keen to accumulate all the status symbols that you can – a bigger house, a better car, for example.

Ladybird

If you doodle a ladybird you are most probably female. You tend to be soft-hearted and romantic and you loathe to hurt anyone. You also have a good sense of humour.

Landscape

Landscape doodles are often done by those who would like to have a baby. A barren landscape can suggest infertility.

The more detailed the landscape, the greater the need to produce a family.

Leaves

Leaf doodles can take many forms; this is a guide to the most common.

1. You are imaginative with a good sense of humour. You also have a very generous nature.

2. You are good-humoured, non-aggressive and take life so easily, you could be described as lazy!

3. You tend to be sarcastic and fussy, and you are easily bogged down with detail.

4. You are feeling weary and/or depressed, which is making you look at everything in a negative manner.

5. Idealistic, you set high standards for others. Your enquiring mind often leads you to seek answers to the inexplicable.

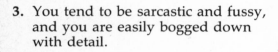

1.

2.

3.

4.

5.

Lightning

A very speedy movement, this, and it shows you are an alert, if impatient, individual. You tend to literally want to change the world 'in a flash'. If something inhibits or restricts you, you will set out to change it. In general, you have a dominant personality.

Lines

A series of straight lines shows a balanced temperament and the ability to stay calm under difficult circumstances. You are reliable and, if the lines rise at one end, enthusiastic.

You are subject to swings of mood – one minute friendly, the next avoiding people. Basically, you are an unreliable character.

Jagged lines show you are suffering from a great deal of inner confusion and the inability to handle day-to-day tasks in a practical manner. You are unable to make-up your mind on any point.

You are subject to feelings of disappointment and frustration. Lines done with very heavy pressure are a sign of aggression too.

Lion

A distinctive doodle, the sign of imagination plus leadership qualities. You like to be in charge and you look for recognition of anything undertaken. Fond of company and very hospitable, you have a generous nature and a good sense of humour. Generally the focus of attention in a crowd, you make an interesting partygoer.

Logos

It is very common for people to doodle over a logo, on a letterhead, for example. Frequently they extend it, enlarge on it or even reshape it.

Adding to a logo shows that you are satisfied and comfortable in your present situation.

Shading in a logo shows you are depressed with the whole situation and wondering about the next move to make.

Distorting a logo shows you are not at all comfortable with the present situation. You suffer general feelings of insecurity and are constantly seeking the right words to express yourself.

Loops

Very full loops show you have excessive emotional needs. You bottle up your feelings because there isn't sufficient outlet for them. When you do let go you are very over-emotional.

Distorted loops indicate you suffer some emotional disturbance and problems in relating to other people.

Narrow loops are the hallmark of an emotionally guarded person. You find free expression of feeling almost impossible.

Lucky Charms

Doodling a four leaf-clover, a wishbone, a horseshoe or a rabbit's foot is normally a sign that you feel in need of a bit of luck. Occasionally such doodles are produced after a run of luck but more often than not the reverse applies. Subconsciously you are saying you could do with all the help you can get.

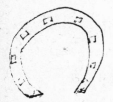 

Luggage

A fairly uncommon one this and
thankfully so. It suggests a parting, a
breaking-up or even passing away.
Normally done when you are feeling
depressed, or after you have been ill for
a long time. (If produced by an elderly
relative, do take time to discuss their
health problems with them.)

Marquee

Normally an indication of a happy
affair, this doodle shows a mixture of
elation and depression. Are you a
parent facing the prospect of the
wedding of your son or daughter to a
partner you do not consider suitable?
Strong feelings of emptiness and
loneliness are exhibited by the side of
the marquee left wide-open.

Masks

You need something to hide behind –
you are a cautious person who does not
fit in with others easily. Guarded about
your ideas, you are often too unsure of
yourself to speak your mind. You have
a tendency to blame others for your
own inadequacies.

Matchbox

The fairly solid construction shows you are the practical type who enjoys working with your hands. There's quite a lot of detail here, indicating you are precise and thorough with anything you produce.

The open box shows you are imaginative, and receptive to the ideas of others.

Maze

Maze-drawing suggests you are feeling trapped. Problems are weighing heavily on your shoulders and you feel you have little chance of escaping your responsibilities. The larger the doodle the greater the feeling of being over-burdened.

Again, you feel you have almost overwhelming problems. But you are also following your intuition and feel you are beginning to see a way out.

Milk Jugs

You have quite a gentle nature but a tendency to be somewhat secretive. There's a lot of emotion hidden under your facade of reserve. Slow to accept change, you are a proud person who needs time to make decisions but will stick with them once taken.

The narrowness of the jug here indicates fear. Often this is well concealed beneath an apparently outgoing personality. You are likely to take offence easily and rarely admit to your true feelings.

Money Signs

You are dissatisfied with your present standard of living. Money gives you a sense of security and feelings of self-worth, and it's on your mind a lot!

(If you work with figures, as an accountant or company secretary for example, these doodles can simply indicate a desire to balance the books.)

Linking money signs together means you love a bargain!

Mountains or Hills

You are ambitious but will work your way up the ladder slowly and cautiously, avoiding any upset to others.

A very determined individual, you believe in success whatever the cost. You do not care who you upset or displace en-route.

That's you at the top – in full control!

Mouth

Lip and mouth doodles have a common theme . . .

Closed lips are a sign of sensuous thoughts. You desire physical contact and make a warm and ardent lover.

Open lips signify a definite 'come-on'! You have a seductive and persuasive personality.

Lips with teeth showing indicate aggressive sexual desires. You are an impatient partner!

A mouth showing gaps in the teeth suggests you love sexual adventure and variety.

A mouth with the tongue sticking out means no one is safe with you – it's straight to bed with no preliminaries!

Mushrooms

Doodling mushrooms is a sign of secretiveness, whatever form they take.

1. You are a tease who invites questions but will not give a straight answer.

2. You become angry if questioned about anything.

3. Basically, you consider your business is your own and you are very cautious with your answers.

  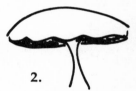

Musical Notes

You are most likely to have a keen interest in music, and a good deal of intuition and sensitivity. If not specifically a music lover, then you like repetitive patterns and show a sense of humour and a certain amount of compulsiveness in your make-up.

Noses

Nose doodles are extremely common and invariably relate to those with a love of material possessions.

A rounded nose indicates a love of showing off your nice home, car, and any trappings of wealth.

The more angular versions indicate you have a great desire to make money. The bigger the nose, the greater the need.

Noughts and crosses

This doodle shows a competitive nature; no matter what sphere of business you are in, you enjoy a challenge. You play to win.

Numbers

A common doodle which shows an interest in money. Constant figure doodling can show a lack of money, or an obsession with it.

Doodling the figure 2 suggests you may feel second rate. (Perhaps you have an elder brother or sister who has achieved a lot with very little effort.)

The figure 1 invariably relates to 'self' and indicates a certain amount of egocentricity.

Ornate Objects

Very embellished objects of any type are the sign of a show-off. You are the sort of person who enjoys regaling a crowd in the pub with dirty stories! If you are male, you will wear a tie with a naked lady on it without batting an eyelid. You have a love of vulgarity and lavatory humour appeals to you.

Ovals

Your attributes of tact and diplomacy help you to achieve your aims; you handle others well. Keeping your own thoughts and position hidden, you always say the right words at the right time.

Again you are tactful and diplomatic; in addition you have learnt how to be direct without being offensive. A good negotiator and quite manipulative.

Pathway

You are a careful, exacting planner who likes 'a place for everything and everything in its place', and you enjoy putting things in order. Gentle and non-aggressive, you take life in your stride and overcome problems as and when they arise.

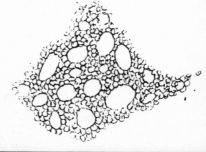

Phallic Symbols

You enjoy deep-thinking and building-up your ideas. Your powers of concentration are quite good and you also handle tricky problems in a clever manner. However, doodles that end up with a phallic symbol on top, indicate your relaxation is undoubtedly sex.

Cacti

These cacti are phallic symbols and more often drawn by women than men. In all cases some frustration is shown by the slightly prickly outlines. Teenagers on the verge of experimenting with sex may well produce them. Likewise unmarried ladies who claim not to want a man around!

Car exhaust

A big exhaust – a true phallic symbol.
You feel good behind the wheel – the
bigger the exhaust and the noisier the
car, the more impressive you feel.
Proud of your 'equipment' in every
sense of the word, you are likely to
prefer one-night stands – these give
you more opportunities to impress
more people!

Lighter

You make no secret of what you are
looking for – you want sex and the
sooner the better. You are rather an
impatient lover who shows little
sensitivity to your partner's needs.
Indeed, heavy pressure indicates a
brutal nature.

Penis

This is a definite feminine doodle.

Women seem uncomfortable doodling a straight-forward penis so they will attempt to disguise it – adding adornments such as bows and funny faces.
These doodles indicate a love of sex and the desire for more sexual activity.

Thumbs

1. A thumb with a shaded nail is a sign you are thoroughly depressed and need comforting. You are longing for warmth, love and affection.

2. You are less depressed but still in need of tender loving care – you need a kindly, sensitive partner to supply your every need! The squareness of the thumb indicates a practical nature – twice a week is sufficient for your needs!

Vegetables

You have a straightforward enjoyment of sex and erotic thoughts. You tend to daydream a lot and invariably have idols on television, or screen, that you fantasise about.

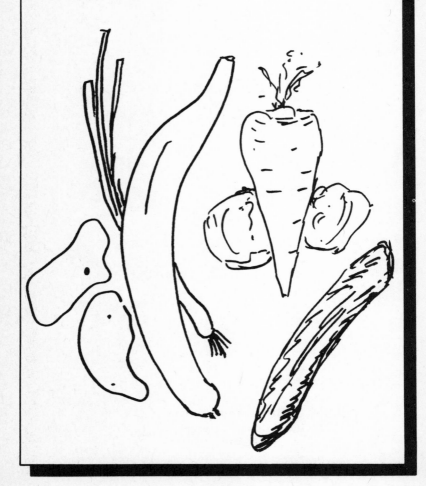

Miscellaneous

You are slightly more obvious in your aims to seduce members of the opposite sex. You like to make it clear in an indirect manner how you would like to behave with someone if you could get them on their own for a while. Although you are the sort of seducer who won't miss a chance, you will not use force to achieve your aims.

Miscellaneous

These doodles indicate preoccupation with sexual thoughts and are often found among the doodles of adolescents. The shading indicates great frustration; you often have strong passions but a poor self-image. Beware of trying to force yourself on an unwilling partner. Heavy pressure, or shading, used in drawing indicates a need to satisfy these strong sexual urges.

Miscellaneous

The corncob, ice cream and train in the tunnel are invariably produced by the fairly shy man who sits and watches ladies in the office while indulging in very erotic thoughts!

You feel you are clever at concealing your thoughts and ideas, which you actually find somewhat embarrassing. You are not likely to discuss your sexual exploits with others.

The equivalent shy female is most likely to doodle the ice cream.

Pictures

The significance of a picture doodle lies in its frame or position, rather than in its subject matter.

In a frame – this shows a cautious attitude. You can only accept gradual change.

Thick, shaded frame – you feel trapped by present circumstances or the environment.

Nailed to the wall – immovable regarding change in status or position, you dig your heels in as a matter of habit.

Spot-lighted – still cautious, you like to give the outward appearance of being very outgoing!

Pig

You are self-conscious and very aware of your self-image. One extra ounce on your frame and you start your next diet! The rounded shape indicates you do not have a lot of willpower, so find it difficult to stick to any particular diet for long.

Pills and Potions

The doodles of a hypochondriac – you are overly anxious about your health – frequently with no real cause.

If the doodle is done low down on the left-hand side of the paper, then your fears are getting out of control and you should seek help. Shading-in shows acute anxiety.

Doodles to the right of the page indicate you are doing your utmost to overcome these fears.

Plants

1. The long, sharp, pointed leaves show you love to criticise others but don't take kindly to criticism yourself. A caustic sense of humour is also evident. The pointed tops also indicate irritation or nervousness; you find it difficult to relax.

2. The roundness here shows a friendly, easy-going nature. You are happiest when you are helping others.

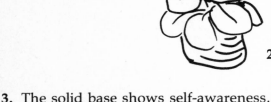

3. The solid base shows self-awareness. The stretched out leaves are evidence of your thirst for knowledge and the retracing shows some insecurity. You are trying to appear more confident than is indeed the case.

Question Marks

This type of doodle is often found on the telephone pad. You like to know other peoples' business and you are very persuasive in finding out what you want to know. A series of question marks show a wish to solve other peoples' problems.

This started out as a simple question mark and then developed from there. It shows you were feeling depressed about your problems initially but then decided you had found the right answer. On the whole you are quite imaginative.

Scales

Produced quite accurately, these show good powers of concentration, attention to detail and a little uncertainty. Basically, you are weighing up the pros and cons in some area which is giving you cause for concern.

A slightly off-balance scale indicates you still have a long way to go in reaching a decision. You are suffering feelings of insecurity.

Sea-shells

The coiled shape shows a desire to be somewhere other than where you are. You are probably a person who needs the odd day off work, or away from home, in order to stand the monotony of your lifestyle. This can make you quite manipulative, in order to achieve your own ends.

Shoes

Shoe doodles always have a sexual connotation.

The rounded top shoe shows an admiration for the female sex but the spiky heel indicates sarcasm.

The pointed toe here means you like ladies, but kept firmly in their place.

A heavier boot and shoe is the sign of a desire to dominate!

Skull & Crossbones

Quite a common doodle and the symbol of the adventurer – someone who wants to spread his interests and activities. You are feeling tied-down at the moment and wondering what the outside world has to offer. Restless, you will try many occupations during your lifetime. Once one interest ceases to stimulate, you move on.

Snails

You are slow, steady and cautious in your thinking, considering every action and every word.

You are trying hard to communicate with others but proceeding cautiously for fear of being misunderstood.

Snowman

The stark, simple lines suggest you are the analytical type who thrives on facts and hates any form of mental embroidery. However, you are quite amiable as long as others stick to the point.

You tend to be slightly narrow-minded, yet retain a dry sense of humour. You like to know where you stand – so directness is appreciated.

Spiders

The heavy shading indicates a great fear of spiders. You are quite likely to scream and run out of the house when you see one! You may even be panic-stricken by harmless, funny representations of spiders – watch out it doesn't develop into a phobia.

Spider's Web

You are quite a tricky customer. An angular drawing shows you like to ensnare or trap others.

The more rounded web can show a feeling of being trapped and seeking a way out.

Both indicate a devious nature and a calculating mind.

Spirals

You have a lot of drive but it's non-aggressive. You operate on the principle of "be nice to others on the way up – you might just meet them on the way down"!

You are quite likely to get to the top of your profession despite your niceness, and your excellent sense of humour will stand you in good stead.

Home and family play an important part in your life.

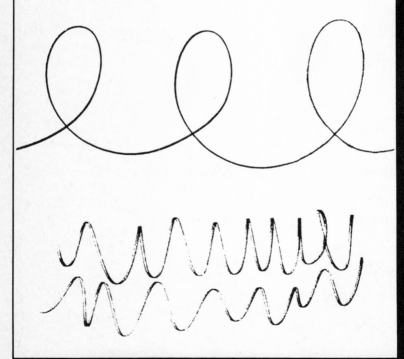

Spiritual Types

These are the doodles of someone with a genial and tolerant nature. The light pressure is a sign of a certain delicacy of feeling, and the subjects a sign of spirituality and idealism.

However, you have difficulty in absorbing experiences and can go on through life repeating your mistakes. You tend to look to others for support, and can be easily dominated by someone stronger.

Squares

Should you produce a number of squares side-by-side but with a little space between, this indicates a solid personality. Not too many surprises come from you.

If you pile them neatly on top of each other, this shows you could have some constructive ability. You are also security conscious!

Squares within squares show you are feeling trapped and are behaving in a somewhat negative manner.

Stairs

Rising stairs show leadership qualities as well as a love of a challenge. You aim to reach the top but are happy to encourage others to follow.

Where the steps fill the whole page your goals are not realistic but are founded in fantasy.

"If at first you don't succeed, try and try again," is your motto. You aren't put off easily and you will make an excellent salesperson.

Stars

A very common doodle which shows quite an aggressive personality. You plan well and intend to reach your goals, which you pursue with dogged determination. Interference by others meets with a strong reaction and when people oppose your ideas, you are always surprised.

A starred circle is the sign of a day-dreamer. You normally look on the bright side of life and you have a pleasant and amiable disposition.

Shading the inside of a star shows you are presenting a cheerful exterior whilst feeling depressed and unhappy inside. You can be quite aggressive if questioned too closely.

Very precise stars indicate an exacting personality. You have a critical and investigative mind which explores and digs for knowledge, always asking questions and seeking answers.

An intellectually thirsty person, you have a great eagerness to learn. The shading does suggest tension which is not too surprising – this example is the doodle of the first female pilot employed by a well-known commercial airline.

Stick Figures

It is usually incorrectly assumed that
this is how children draw themselves or
their parents. These are adult-type
doodles and if you produce these you
like to come straight to the point. Good
at recognising the essentials and acting
upon them, you are analytical, like facts
and have a great distrust of mental
embroidery.

Such simple figures tend to indicate
high intelligence and can reflect the
doodler's inner harmony.

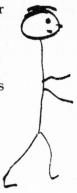

Sun

An equal amount of sun and cloud signify you are experiencing feelings of conflict and are uncertain how to handle your problems.

A large sun and smaller cloud show you are overcoming your problems and feeling a great deal happier.

A small sun and a large cloud – you have allowed your problems to overwhelm you and are generally feeling pretty miserable.

Brilliant sunshine – life is looking good and you are full of hope

Syringe

The sign of a very sharp, sarcastic personality – you like to subdue others with a few well-chosen words. You have an alert, analytical mind, and you like to get to the core of everything, but you lack humour, tending to be clinical, cold and unemotional.

Tables

These doodles show a practical nature. You are earthy, methodical and stubborn. You may also have a strong materialistic streak and an attachment to all tangible goods.

Communicating your needs to others does not come easily to you, nor can you easily understand what others require of you.

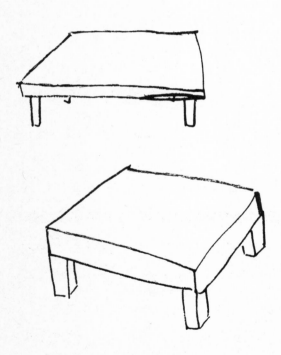

Tea Cup

An elaborate doodle, with a great deal of touching-up and amending. You are likely to be quite an irritable person who finds difficulty in expressing yourself. When others do not immediately understand your ideas you feel very frustrated. Impractical by nature, you have a rather shy personality.

Telephone

You love communicating, but you are slightly impatient and tend to blurt out the first thought that comes to mind. Tact is not your strong point but at least others know what you are thinking.

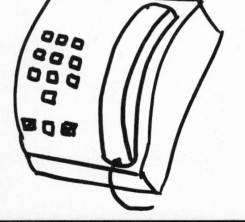

The phone placed neatly in position and the drawing of the whole instrument indicates a more practical nature as well as a good communicator. You do not waste words, but come straight to-the-point.

Tents

A securely pegged-down tent shows
you are the cautious type who likes
everything on a firm footing. You
respond to logic but are immune to
emotional appeals.

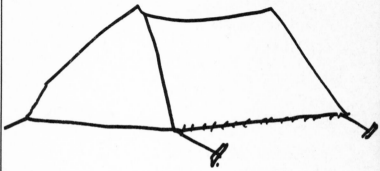

The sign of a much more frivolous
nature – you are good humoured,
romantic (as shown by the flowers),
and always welcoming to guests.

Tophat and Tails

An escapist with the distinct tendency to run from problems, you are pleasant to know as long as relationships are kept on a light-hearted note.

Torture instruments

Doodling such things is a sign you are wishing ill-will or actual physical harm to others. You may have just suffered a break-up in a relationship and taken it very hard indeed. In your depressed frame of mind you have a strong desire to retaliate against feelings of pain or rejection – either real or imaginary.

Luckily, these doodles are normally of a temporary nature, but if they are produced habitually – watch out!

Traffic Lights

A great 'doer' and always on-the-go, efficiency is your motto. Slightly curt and always to-the-point, you have a strong dislike of petty rules and regulations.

A 'touchy' individual, you like to be active but feel others deliberately slow you down. You work hard despite obstacles.

Trees

Doodling a rounded tree bearing fruit shows you are a warm-hearted and friendly person. A well-balanced individual, you have a good sense of humour.

This uncoordinated type of tree shows an impulsive nature. You do things in haste but worry at leisure.

A nicely rounded tree – you are reliable, friendly and your friends look forward to having you round – that is if you haven't already invited them to your home.

Christmas tree – you are sarcastic and can be aggressive under pressure. A very fussy character!

The willow – you are feeling either very tired or depressed today. Nothing is quite as black as you see it at the moment.

Tree in winter – impatience is in evidence here. You are very critical of others but loathe criticism yourself.

Upright, shaded trunk – this is the sign of the loner, often with an inferiority complex.

Triangles

An indication of a constructive mind and a practical approach. You are probably a loner who can concentrate for long periods of time alone on a project. The approval of others is not necessary to you and you are basically individualistic. An intellectually thirsty person with an eagerness to learn, you can be quite perverse!

This elaborate triangle shows a probing mind. You started off in quite a depressed frame of mind but as the doodle progressed upwards, you felt you had found the answer to your problems. A very intelligent person you positively enjoy solving problems.

Another answer-seeker – the shading shows depression, while the curved, extended lines show you are broadening your range of vision.

Tubes

Doodles of this type show a practical approach to any task undertaken but difficulty in getting down to tasks in hand. The clear, straight lines show clarity of thought, but the roundedness is a sign that you tend to be lazy.

There is a dislike of friction or any form of pressure shown here. A flexible personality, you try to see all points of view.

Umbrellas

The rounded top indicates you have a secretive side to your nature. You find difficulty in enjoying life to the full as you rarely say exactly what you mean and can easily end up feeling hurt and misunderstood.

The closed umbrella suggests secretiveness and difficulty in communicating; you often feel "nobody understands me".

Vases

A vase with a single flower is a sign of purposefulness and maturity. It also shows intelligence, a dislike of clutter and an eye for the essential. You probably have a strong dislike of vulgarity or loud effects.

A nicely arranged vase of flower shows the orderly, imaginative and practically creative mind. You are outgoing, expansive and comfortable with others, but may have a tendency to over-indulge in the good things in life!

The rather messy flower vase suggests you are disorganised, easy-going and not easily embarrassed. Charming and hospitable you certainly are, but your visitors are likely to have to move half a dozen objects before they can sit down!

Waves

This is a very gentle movement and shows a lover of peace. You hate anger or aggression of any kind and will attempt to settle all problems in a conciliatory manner. Positive decisions do not come easily to you.

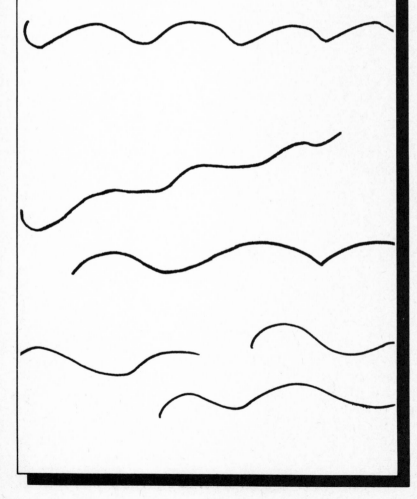

Weapons

These are all sharp instruments but doodled with a lighter pressure. They indicate callousness, a desire to inflict pain on others and a cold, undemonstrative personality.

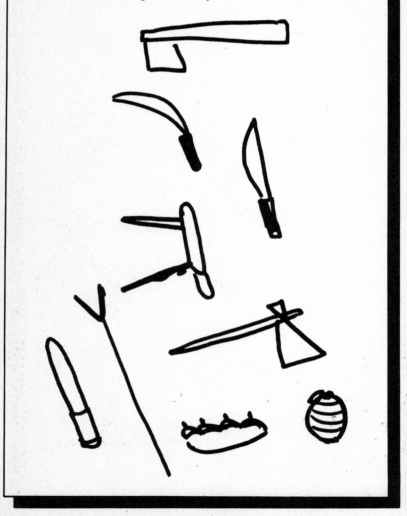

Weapons

These heavy pressure doodles show extreme bad temper and the strong possibility of violence. If you produce something like this, you probably have excessive energy without sufficient outlet, and are subject to very explosive outbursts.

People who produce such doodles as a habit are very likely to commit crimes. Just a very occasional one can show a temporary feeling of great anger.

Wheels

Frustration is shown in these doodles – you are limited by circumstances and want to break free from your ties. You may feel that because of your situation you are not able to fully exploit your personality.

You feel encumbered and hindered by others – the mudguard suggests you can see no way out.

Whips

You have a strong cruel streak and a desire to lash out – either physically or mentally.

X-ing

X's of any type are a sign of feelings of martyrdom and guilt. You may have strong religious feelings, or perhaps you have been deeply touched by a recent death. This could be of a loved one or even someone you greatly admired.

Although you fear death, you are also attracted by it.

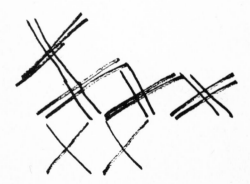

Yo-yo

These doodles are the product of those who enjoy a challenge – the feeling of movement suggests that something is happening. You will push your ideas until they are accepted, and the more angular the yo-yo the greater the effort you put in.

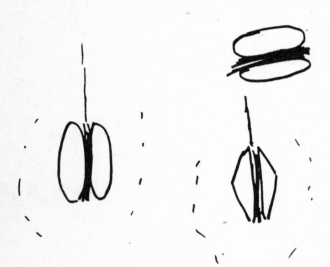

Zig-zags

The sign of a determined personality.
Rising zig zags show you do not like to
be held back.

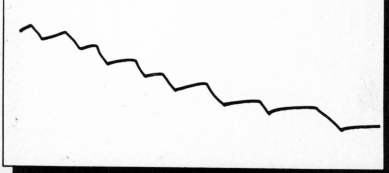

If the zig-zags tend to fall at the end
then you feel you are not getting far
enough and you may well resort to
stronger tactics.